To

From

Date

FRIENDS

PHOTOGRAPHY COPYRIGHT © 1996 BY VIRGINIA DIXON

TEXT COPYRIGHT © 1996 BY GARBORG'S HEART 'N HOME, INC.

DESIGN BY MICK THURBER

PUBLISHED BY GARBORG'S HEART 'N HOME, INC.

P.O. BOX 20132, BLOOMINGTON, MN 55420

❧

❧

JANET L. WEAVER WISHES TO THANK JOAN M. GARBORG FOR HER EDITORIAL
DIRECTION AND WENDY GREENBERG FOR HER "APPLES OF GOLD."

ISBN 1-88130-29-4

Friends

Photography by Virginia Dixon with featured sentiments by Janet L. Weaver

To have a friend is to have one of the

sweetest gifts that life can bring.

....

AMY ROBERTSON BROWN

I thank God for the blessing you are…for the joy

of your laughter…the comfort of your prayers…

the warmth of your smile.

Thoughtfulness is to friendship what sunshine

is to a garden.

The sweetest roses of my heart bloom in the garden of our friendship.

A friend likes
everything
about you, even
the things you
try not to show.

A friend listens with her eyes and her heart…and understands what you can't put into words.

Friendship is not created by what we give, but more by what we share. It makes a whole world of things easier to bear.

Every true friend is a glimpse of God.

LUCY LARCOM

Favorite people, favorite places,

favorite memories of the past…

These are the joys of a lifetime…

these are the things that last.

A friend is what the heart needs all the time.

....

HENRY VAN DYKE

The discovery of friendship is well worth the search.

*The best
friendships
often come in
unexpected
packages.*

Someone to talk to, to laugh with, to tell secrets to…

I'm just so thankful for the friend I've found in you.

Everything I do is twice as nice with you!

Happiness is my friend's hand.

....

GILLIAN QUEEN, AGE 10

If I had a single flower for every time I think about you,

I could walk forever in my garden.

....

CLAUDIA A. GRANDI

Little kindnesses, little acts of considerateness, little

appreciations, little confidences…are all that are

needed to keep a friendship sweet.

....

HUGH BLACK

Our
friendship
has a rare
and lovely
fragrance.

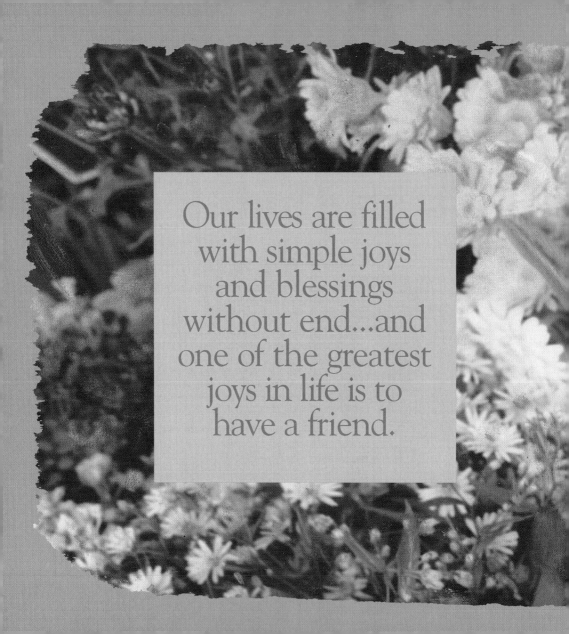

Our lives are filled
with simple joys
and blessings
without end...and
one of the greatest
joys in life is to
have a friend.

I will always keep
the memory of the
special joys we have
shared close to my
heart.

Joy is the echo of God's life within us.

....

JOSEPH MARMION

In your presence is fullness of joy; at your right hand are

pleasures forevermore.

....

PSALM 16:11 NKJV

Thank you for the treasure of your friendship…

for showing me God's special heart of love.

God's friendship is the unexpected joy we find when we reach His outstretched hand.

*Friends splash
our world with
sunny color
and set our
hearts to flight.*

Friends are the sunshine of life.

When friends meet, hearts warm.

....

JOHN RAY

One of the highest compliments I can receive is

that I am your friend.

There is an exquisite melody in every heart. If we listen

closely, we can hear each other's song. A friend knows the

song in your heart and responds with beautiful harmony.

Your kindness gives love a melody, your friendship

gives memory a tune.

Friendship is the cadence of divine melody melting

through the heart.

MILDMAY

*The song of
our friendship is
a melody only
our hearts
can sing.*

It's nice to know there is someone you can tell everything to, and they'll still like you when you're done.

A friend is one who knows all about you

and won't go away.

What the heart gives away is never lost…it is kept in the

hearts of others.

A friend loves at all times.

PROVERBS 17:17 NKJV

Sometimes the friends we've searched so hard for were right behind us all the time.

Being with you is like walking on a very clear morning—

definitely the sensation of belonging there.

....

E. B. WHITE

A friend is the hope of the heart.

....

RALPH WALDO EMERSON

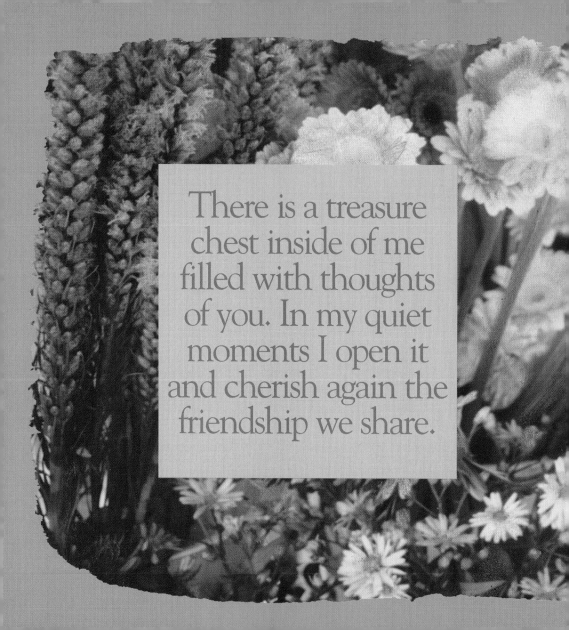

There is a treasure chest inside of me filled with thoughts of you. In my quiet moments I open it and cherish again the friendship we share.

Meeting someone
for the first time
is like going on a
treasure hunt.
What wonderful
worlds we can find
in others!

EDWARD E. FORD

We have been friends together in sunshine and in shade.

....

CAROLINE E. S. NORTON

Hold a true friend with both your hands.

Friendship is sharing openly, laughing often, trusting always, caring deeply.

When I feel uncertain, your friendship reminds me that some things in life are constant.

*Our
friendship
is a
perfect fit.*

Together is the nicest place to be.

Now may the warming love of friends

surround you as you go

Down the path of light and laughter where

the happy memories grow.

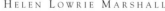

HELEN LOWRIE MARSHALL